THE BIG GREEN BOOK

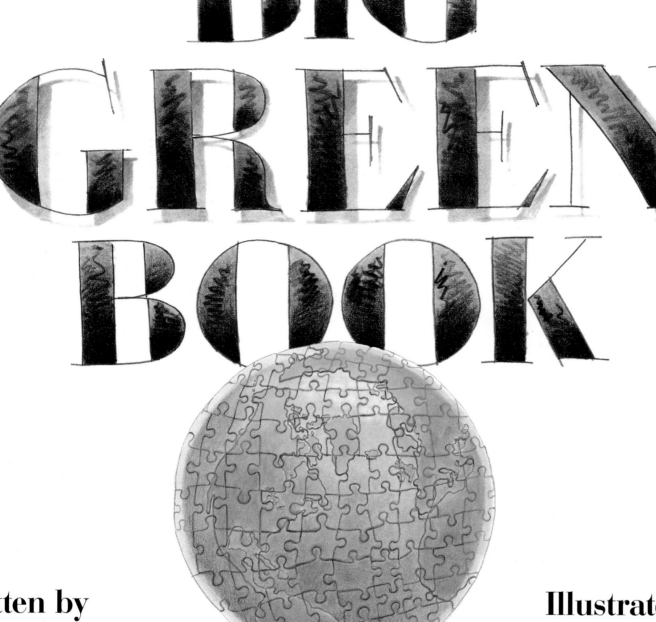

Written by
Fred Pearce

Illustrated by
Ian Winton

Foreword by
James Lovelock

Publishers · GROSSET & DUNLAP · *New York*

FOREWORD

In many ways Earth is like a living thing — not quite alive like you and me, but alive all the same. Like our breath and blood, the air and all the waters of the world keep Earth nourished and healthy.

What would Earth be like if it were dead? It would be like Mars or Venus or the Moon, just bone-dry bare rock — either roasting hot as on Venus or freezing cold as on Mars — with not a drop of water and no life-giving oxygen in the air.

We are so lucky to have Earth, which has been a warm and comfortable home to all kinds of living creatures for 4 billion years. I have come to call our living planet Gaia, after the Greek goddess of the Earth. The name Gaia also refers to my theory which seeks to explain why the Earth is nearly always comfortable for all its inhabitants.

I hope that you will enjoy THE BIG GREEN BOOK as much as I did. This book will help you understand why our Earth is such a special place; what the dangers are to our planet; and how all of us must work to keep Earth safe and healthy for our children and our children's children and for all generations to come.

James E Lovelock.

CONTENTS

THE GOLDILOCKS PLANET

Earth is one of nine planets that circle the Sun. So far as we know, Earth is the only planet that is home to living things. Earth and its nearest neighbors, Mars and Venus, were formed at the same time, in the same way, and from the same sort of rocks. So why is there life on Earth but nowhere else?

One reason is the heat from the Sun — what we call sunlight. Without it, neither plants nor animals could live. Venus is much closer to the Sun than Earth, and it receives much more heat. The temperature on the surface of Venus is over 842°F (450° C), hotter than a kitchen oven at its hottest. Mars and the other planets further away from the Sun receive much less heat than Earth. Living on Mars would be like living inside a freezer — very, very cold.

Like the bowl of porridge that Goldilocks ate in the story of the Three Bears, the temperature on Earth is not too hot, not too cold, but just right for life.

Neptune

Jupiter

Saturn

Mars

Mercury

Venus

Sun

Earth

Moon

Venus is too hot

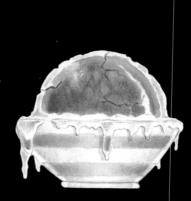

Mars is too cold

but Earth is just right

Uranus

Carbon dioxide acts like an invisible blanket, holding in some of the heat from the Sun.

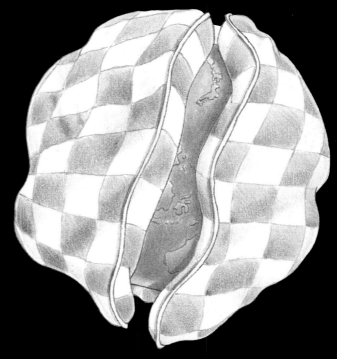

The atmosphere, the thick layer of gases that surrounds our planet, is another reason for life on Earth. It is made up mostly of nitrogen, some oxygen and a little carbon dioxide and water vapor. We use oxygen to breathe, but carbon dioxide is also essential for life on Earth. It acts like a blanket wrapped around the planet, absorbing some of the heat from the Sun. Venus has a very thick blanket of carbon dioxide that keeps it very hot. Mars has very little carbon dioxide to keep the heat in. If Earth had no atmosphere, it would be like Mars — freezing cold, with a temperature of around -4°F (-20°C).

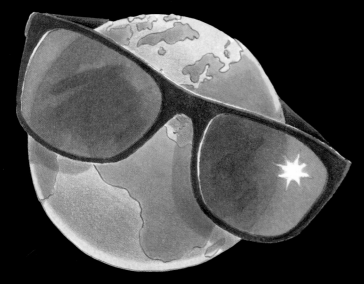

Although we need the Sun to live, some of its rays are harmful to us. Strong, invisible rays, called ultraviolet radiation, cause sunburn and can increase our chances of getting skin cancer and other diseases. But part of our atmosphere, high above Earth, protects us by blocking out most of the harmful ultraviolet radiation. We call this part of the atmosphere the ozone layer. No living thing on the surface of our planet could survive without the protection of the ozone layer.

The ozone layer acts like a pair of sunglasses, blocking out harmful ultraviolet radiation.

A BUMPY RIDE

Earth was formed about 5 billion years ago. The first living things on it were tiny organisms on the bottom of the oceans. They appeared about 4 billion years ago. Living things have not always found it easy to survive on Earth. But, like a spinning top, the planet has recovered every time it has been knocked off balance.

The first tiny living things on Earth probably formed in a gooey "soup" on the bottom of the oceans, perhaps 4 billion years ago.

About 2 billion years ago, some tiny floating plants called algae began to make oxygen. Oxygen collected in the oceans. Then it started to bubble up out of the water and, for the first time, there was oxygen in the atmosphere. The algae changed the atmosphere of Earth.

Many of the tiny organisms in the oceans were killed by oxygen. It was poisonous to them. But the oxygen allowed others, including those that produced the oxygen, to grow and evolve. Sunlight turned some of the oxygen in the air into ozone, which is a special form of oxygen. With oxygen to breathe and an ozone layer for protection from harmful rays from the Sun, the first plants and animals moved ashore less than a billion years ago.

Less than a billion years ago, living things moved from water onto land.

Several times in Earth's history, there have been natural catastrophes. Every few million years, comets hurtle towards our planet from the far side of our galaxy. Occasionally, they crash into Earth.

The biggest comet may have crashed into our planet 250 million years ago. The crash seems to have made the oceans boil and huge fires rage. Most types of living things died out. But within a few million years, the atmosphere and the oceans recovered, and entirely new types of animals, including the predecessors of dinosaurs, evolved.

8

Comets the size of cities have crashed into Earth several times.

Another comet may have hit Earth 65 million years ago. Many scientists think that it set the planet on fire and killed off half of all living things, including dinosaurs. Many small animals survived, however. They evolved over millions of years into the animals — human beings included — that we know today.

Humanlike creatures first walked on Earth about 2 million years ago. It was about then that a slight wobble in the planet's orbit around the Sun started the first Ice Age. Sheets of ice spread out from the North Pole until they covered large parts of the planet, including where cities such as London, New York, and Berlin now stand. Eventually, the ice retreated. But the wobble has caused several Ice Ages since then, and each time the ice has killed off many types of plants and animals. In a few thousand years' time, your home might be buried beneath a layer of ice several miles thick.

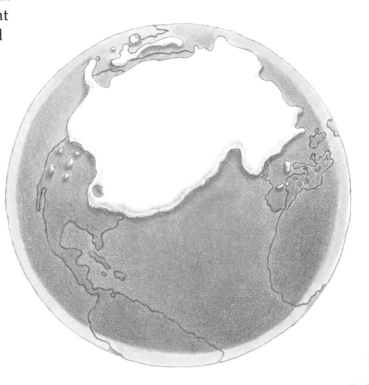

About 2 million years ago, a slight wobble in Earth's orbit around the Sun caused ice sheets to spread across the planet.

Despite Earth's bumpy ride through time, our planet has always remained a place where life can survive. But today, life on Earth may be facing its greatest threat from one of its newest creatures — human beings.

Modern man casts a long shadow across the future of living things on Earth.

9

THE GREAT BALANCING ACT

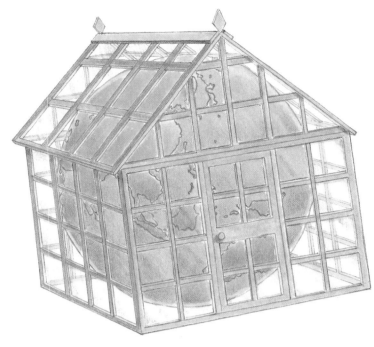

Millions of years ago, the atmosphere was very different from the way it is today. There was no oxygen, and the atmosphere was composed almost entirely of carbon dioxide. The carbon dioxide and other gases trapped enough of the Sun's heat to keep Earth warm. These gases are known as greenhouse gases, because they hold in heat from the Sun, rather like the panes of glass in a greenhouse.

Like the glass windows in a greenhouse, gases, such as carbon dioxide, trap the Sun's heat and keep us warm.

When it first formed, our atmosphere was 98% carbon dioxide.

When the atmosphere first formed, the Sun was not nearly as hot as it is today. So you might expect that the temperature on Earth would have been freezing cold. In fact, scientists have found evidence from fossils of living things from 3 billion years ago that shows that the climate was more or less the same as it is now.

How has the climate stayed so stable? The secret may lie with the greenhouse gases. When the Sun was cooler, the atmosphere was 98% carbon dioxide. But as the Sun has gradually become hotter, the amount of carbon dioxide in the air has decreased dramatically to less than 1% today. It's as if Earth has been able to shed several layers of thick blankets to keep its temperature constant. But where has all the carbon dioxide gone?

Today it is less than 1% carbon dioxide.

Over hundreds of millions of years the carbon dioxide in the planet's early atmosphere has been absorbed by living things, especially those in the oceans. They use the carbon to grow and make tissue and skeletons. When they die, their remains fall to the ocean floor where, eventually, they form new rock. Living things have always played an important role in controlling the planet's temperature. Without them, there would be much more carbon dioxide in the air — and our planet would be much hotter.

Living things keep our environment fit for life by controlling the amount of chemicals in the air and water. They keep the amount of salt in the oceans from rising too high. They also keep a constant control on oxygen in the air. For hundreds of millions of years, roughly a quarter of our atmosphere has been made up of oxygen. If the amount rose, fires would quickly spread across the planet. This is because fires burn much faster where there is more oxygen. But if there were much less oxygen, most living things, including humans, would suffocate.

Oxygen is constantly being destroyed in the air by sunlight. But it is replaced by plants, which manufacture oxygen. Without plants, the atmosphere would soon run out of oxygen.

By absorbing carbon dioxide from the air, the oceans have acted like a thermostat, keeping the world at the right temperature.

Our atmosphere performs a constant balancing act. Too much oxygen and we would all burn up . . . too little and we would suffocate.

THE HUMAN FOOTPRINT

Modern man, known as Homo sapiens, evolved about 40,000 years ago, during the last Ice Age. About 10,000 years ago, man began to tame and alter the environment by planting crops, keeping animals, and building towns and cities. At that time, the world population was about 10 million. Since then, it has increased fairly steadily, but it surges occasionally when humans find new ways to feed more people. Over the past 250 years, the population has grown from 500 million to around 5 billion people.

Imagine humans as a load pulled by an engine, called Earth. When there were only a few million humans, the engine had no problem. But now it has 5 billion people to pull and its fuel may be running low.

ACQUIRED BY MANKIND Inc.

Even though the current population increase is beginning to slow down, scientists estimate that there will be 10 billion people on the planet by the year 2100. Each year there are another 80 million people on Earth, all needing food and shelter. When fewer people were cutting down trees for fuel, diverting rivers to water fields, and mining the land, there was little damage to the environment. Now that humans have taken over most of the available land, the damage is worldwide. There are human footprints wherever we look — roads through rainforests, oil rigs in the Arctic, and cattle ranchers' fences where animals were once free to roam. As people take over land for farms and cities, they destroy plants and animals.

Homo sapiens is taking over the planet. There are very few untouched places left, such as the middle of rainforests, deserts, and Antarctica.

More and more roads are built to link towns, ports, and countries. They often crisscross untouched land.

Farmers need to grow more and more food to feed all the billions of people. Recently, scientists have developed new types of grain which ripen more quickly and produce more food. But these crops need fertilizers to grow well and pesticides to kill off pests and prevent disease. These chemicals, in turn, upset the natural balance of insects and animals which live on and around the crops.

Farmers now grow twice as much food as they did thirty years ago.

The pesticides and fertilizers that farmers use interfere with the chemistry of soils. The farmers may get a bumper crop for a few years, but in time even the best fields may turn into deserts.

In many places, soils have lost their natural goodness, because farmers plow their land year after year to increase the amount of food that they grow. Eventually the soil becomes like dust and is blown away by wind or washed away by rain. In the highlands of Ethiopia, farmers lose an estimated 3 billion tons of soil each year.

When farmers overuse their land, the top layer of fertile soil starts to peel away.

13

Most of Earth's resources are used by enormous megacities, each with over 10 million inhabitants — more than the entire population of the whole world just 10,000 years ago. By the year 2000, there will be more than twenty-five megacities and almost half of the world population will be city dwellers. Particularly in poor countries, thousands of people move into these cities each year, hoping to find work. Most don't and end up living without proper housing, water supplies or sewage systems.

Earth pays a terrible price trying to feed, clothe, and house all the people in these megacities. Mexico City, the world's largest city, may look like a tiny spot on a map of Mexico, but its 19 million inhabitants eat more than half the food produced in all of Mexico. Three-quarters of the people in China live in the country, but big cities like Beijing use three-quarters of the country's electricity.

Megacities are growing all over the world.

Land is destroyed to provide building materials, fuel, and metals for the megacities.

Megacities have nowhere to put waste except in the surrounding countryside.

As megacities grow, wild animals flee and countryside is destroyed.

14

WATER - THE SPRING OF LIFE

It is curious that we called our planet "Earth" when, in fact, over 70% of it is covered with water. Water is essential to life. Without it neither plants nor animals could survive. But almost all the world's water is in the oceans, where it is salty and of little use to humans. Less than 3% is fresh water and most of that is frozen in the polar ice caps or glaciers. Amazingly, less than 1% of the world's water is found in rivers, lakes, or underground, where we can make use of it.

There will never be any more fresh water than there is now. The water we use is recycled over and over again. As the Sun heats the seas and lakes, millions of gallons of water rise into the air as invisible water vapor. This is known as evaporation. As the vapor rises, it cools and turns back into water droplets, forming clouds. The droplets join together — this is called condensation — and fall back as rain. The rain runs off the land into rivers, which eventually flow back into the sea, and the cycle is repeated.

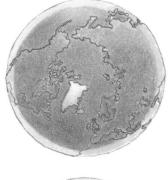

Most of the world is covered by water.

The natural water cycle

clouds form

rain falls

water flows back to the sea

water evaporates

This natural plumbing system is absolutely vital for life on Earth, yet we are poisoning more and more of this precious fresh water by pouring dangerous pollutants into rivers. When the water evaporates into the air, the pollution is left behind. Human sewage is a major pollutant, particularly in many parts of Africa, Asia, and South America, where people use the same water for washing, drinking, and as a toilet. Human sewage contains bacteria and viruses that cause deadly diseases. Although many countries treat sewage to make it less dangerous, in other places, untreated sewage is poured directly into rivers or the sea.

More and more of our precious freshwater supply is being polluted.

Water is polluted in many other ways. Industrial waste is often poured deliberately into rivers. It may also leak accidentally from garbage dumps or underground storage tanks. Rain often washes pesticides into rivers. These chemicals seep through the soil to natural underground reservoirs of pure drinking water. If this water is polluted, the poisons stay there forever. Some cities are now spending billions of dollars to clean up water made unsafe by such pollution.

Dangerous metals, such as mercury and lead, have been buried underground. These waste dumps are like toxic time bombs, because no one knows when their poison will seep into the underground reservoirs from which millions of people take their drinking water.

Dams allow the flow of water to be controlled. They provide a store of water and can help prevent flooding.

Over the last fifty years, people have built dams across some of the world's largest rivers. The water behind a dam forms a lake. Although dams have been useful for generating electricity and watering the land to grow crops, they have also caused problems. Before they were dammed, the rivers brought fine soil, called silt, downstream from the mountains. The silt naturally fertilized the land each year when the rivers flooded. Dams prevent the silt from flowing downstream, so that the farmers there have to buy artificial fertilizer.

Rivers also carry salt from mountain rocks. Normally they carry the salt straight into the sea. When a dam diverts the water onto fields, the crops absorb the water, leaving the salt in the soil. Crops cannot grow in salty soil, so scientists are now looking at ways to wash the soil clean and to develop plants that can tolerate salt.

In parts of India, Pakistan, Mexico, and the United States, fields are now covered with a white crust of salt and are useless for growing crops.

For a long time, people thought it didn't matter how much waste was dumped in the oceans. They believed the oceans were so big that the waste would disperse harmlessly. Now they know better. Many coastal waters, where the water is shallow and rich in marine life, are becoming contaminated with sewage, chemicals and garbage. Leaks from oil tankers can leave a thin slick of oil, many miles across, on the surface of the ocean.

Poisoning the water cycle

Rain washes nitrates from fertilizers into rivers and seas. These, in turn, fertilize the water, so that algae grow more quickly. The increase in algae eventually kills off fish.

Factories near rivers dump oil, metals, and chemicals into the water, which can poison wildlife.

Untreated human sewage is often poured into rivers and coastal waters.

Dolphins, seals, and whales may become poisoned when they feed on fish which are already contaminated by pollution.

Millions of tons of plastics, which may take centuries to disintegrate, have been thrown into the sea. Birds and sea animals often swallow the plastic or get caught in it and die.

Pesticides can pollute water in rivers or underground reservoirs, making it undrinkable.

Every year up to 10 million tons of oil leak from tankers crossing the oceans. Oil slicks block out sunlight, disrupting the food chain. Luckily, bacteria slowly eat the oil, otherwise many oceans would be covered in oil.

Pollution has reached even such remote places as Antarctica. Lead and acid from rain have been trapped in the ice, and DDT, a powerful pesticide, has been found in the bodies of seals, penguins, and other polar animals.

THE WORLD IN A TRASH CAN

Every human contributes to the state of our planet. Some people, however, do far more damage than others. People who live in rich, industrialized countries consume most of the world's limited resources: they mine more metals to make everything from cars to soda cans; they burn more oil to run their cars; they use more gas and electricity to light and heat their homes; they eat more food and chop down more forests for wood and paper. A quarter of the world's people consume three-quarters of the world's resources. The United States alone burns a quarter of the world's coal and oil each year, and uses more than a quarter of the world's aluminum and copper.

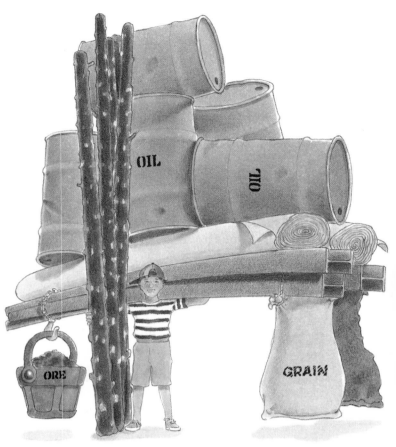

One child in an industrialized country consumes as much as ten children in a poorer country, so a child born in a rich country is a far bigger burden on the planet.

A typical family may produce 100 pounds (50 kg) of rubbish every week. That's more than 2 tons a year.

In the "throw-away societies" of Europe and North America, most waste is poured down the drain, thrown on the street, or left out for the garbage truck. More than a third of what we throw away is paper or cardboard. In our lifetime, each of us may throw away 50 tons of trash, including paper made from more than 200 trees.

People who live in the countryside of poor countries produce virtually no waste at all. They mainly eat the food they grow — they don't buy packaged food. Any leftovers are used to fertilize the next year's crop. People who live in the cities of these countries, however, now have similar throw-away habits to the industrialized world and create huge garbage dumps. Some poor city dwellers make a living scavenging through these dumps for things to sell.

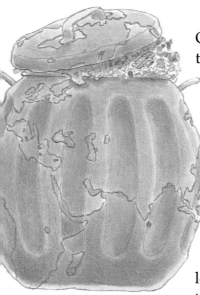

Our planet is littered with more and more trash. Everywhere that people go, they leave litter behind them. Just think — a soda can thrown thoughtlessly out of a car may still be there 500 years from now if no one else comes to pick it up. All the waste people create has to go somewhere. Usually it is either burned or buried. Many countries are now running out of places where they can safely bury their garbage and scientists are worried about the effects of dangerous chemicals that are released when waste is burned. Some cities now load their garbage aboard ships and send it to other countries or dump it at sea.

Earth has become our trash can . . .

. . . the rivers and oceans have become our drain.

Most of us don't think about where our waste goes — as long as it goes. It's like brushing dust under the carpet.

To solve the trash crisis, we all need to recycle garbage whenever possible. Glass bottles, aluminum cans and newspapers can all be sent back to factories and turned into new bottles, cans, and paper. This means that less waste is produced and we save on raw materials.

Almost everything can be recycled — paper, aluminum, cardboard, glass, cans, old clothes, leftover food. If it can't be recycled, ask yourself: Do I really need it?

RUINING THE RAINFOREST

Until less than 100 years ago, most of the countries that straddle the equator were covered with vast, wet, steamy forests, known as rainforests. Rainforests are among nature's greatest triumphs. They cover only 6% of the land, but they are home to more than half of all the types of plants and animals on Earth, perhaps as many as 15 million species. Millions of people live in rainforests as well. Most of the inhabitants still live very simply, hunting animals such as wild pigs and cutting small clearings to plant crops. But their land is being taken over by outsiders who are clearing the land for crops, timber companies who are cutting down and selling the hardwood trees, and cattle ranchers. The destruction of the rainforests could be a disaster both for nature and for the people who live in the forests.

Indicates the regions of tropical rainforests.

Trees are like giant sponges soaking up vast amounts of rainwater. Some water evaporates in the hot sun. The rest passes through the trees to the soil.

Plant roots keep moisture in the soil and hold the soil particles in place.

A rainforest is a giant water and weather machine. It needs a lot of rain to grow, but it also creates rain by continually recycling water. Water is stored in the soil, in the trees, and even in the air.

When rain falls in a rainforest, most of it lands on the leaves.

The heat of the Sun makes the raindrops evaporate into the air.

The raindrops are blown many miles, then form new clouds that rain again on the forest.

20

The rainforest is a complex balance of plants and animals. Each one has its own part to play in the balance of nature. The rainforest is like a stack of cans in a supermarket. The trees and animals which the inhabitants use are like the cans at the top. If they are removed, they do not harm the rest.

The main forest is like the cans at the bottom. If they are removed, the whole stack tumbles down. If the forest is cut down, the people, plants, and animals in it are destroyed.

If the trees are removed, the rain falls to the ground and runs into rivers and the sea. It often washes away the forest soils that were held in place by the tree roots. If there are fewer trees to recycle the water, there will be less rain, and the soil will become drier.

Rainforests play an important role in rainfall, not just over the rainforests but over the entire planet. Scientists fear that if we chop down much more of the very large rainforests in Brazil and Central Africa, the climate may change all over the world.

Every second of every minute of every hour of every day, an area of rainforest the size of a soccer field is destroyed. Every day one species of animal, insect, or plant disappears forever.

Cutting down the trees is like pulling a giant plug in the rainmaking cycle. Without trees to store the water, it is lost.

We have found many plants in the rainforests useful as foods or medicines. There may be thousands more waiting to be discovered, but because the rainforests are being destroyed at such a fast rate, we may never find them.

21

THE GREENHOUSE EFFECT

The destruction of the rainforests is changing the balance of gases in the atmosphere. Trees absorb carbon dioxide as they grow. But when they are burned or rot after being cut down, they release carbon dioxide. If carbon dioxide is released faster than it can be absorbed, there will be more carbon dioxide in the air. This will trap more heat from the Sun and add to Earth's natural greenhouse effect.

Burning fossil fuels — oil, coal, and gas — also releases carbon dioxide into the atmosphere. These fuels are the remains of ancient forests that grew tens of millions of years ago.

Every tree, every ton of coal or oil, contains within it trapped carbon. When burned, the carbon is released into the atmosphere as carbon dioxide — just as a balloon releases gas when popped.

About 200 years ago, the first large factories were built and began spewing out carbon dioxide. Since then, the amount of carbon dioxide in the atmosphere has increased by a third.

Earth is in flames. Every year, farmers set the rainforests on fire to clear land to farm. And in industrialized countries, power plants and cars release even more carbon dioxide.

Special sorts of bacteria produce methane. They are found in marshes and bogs, in paddy fields, in garbage dumps, and in the guts of cattle and sheep. Natural gas also contains methane.

Humans have also increased the amount of other "greenhouse gases" in the atmosphere. One of these is methane. This gas is produced by bugs that live in garbage dumps, in wet places such as waterlogged rice fields, and in the guts of cattle and sheep. As the world grows more rice, raises more cattle, and creates more garbage dumps, the amount of methane in the air increases. It has doubled in the past 200 years.

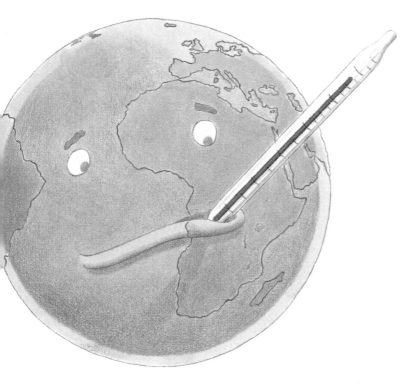

CFCs are used either in the making of these things, or to help them work.

Man-made chemicals called chlorofluorocarbons, or CFCs for short, are a third source of greenhouse gases. They have been used in refrigerators, air conditioners, foam plastics and, until recently, in aerosol spray cans.

As these greenhouse gases build up in the atmosphere, they trap more heat. The result is that the world is likely to become hotter. Scientists call this global warming. It may already be under way. The 1980s were the warmest decade on record around the world. If greenhouse gases are added to the atmosphere at the present ever-rising rate, the global temperature could rise by 7°F (4°C) by the year 2030.

Like a human on a hot summer's day, Earth is overheating.

A WARMER WORLD

Y ou may think that a temperature rise of 7°F (4°C) worldwide would be nothing much to worry about. However, a drop of 7°F would be enough to take us back to an Ice Age. A rise of 7°F would make the Earth warmer than it has been for the last 100,000 years and would upset the world's climate. Climatologists (people who study the weather) have gathered enough information about changing rainfall and temperatures from around the world to agree that the world is getting warmer. But they cannot be sure how this will affect our planet.

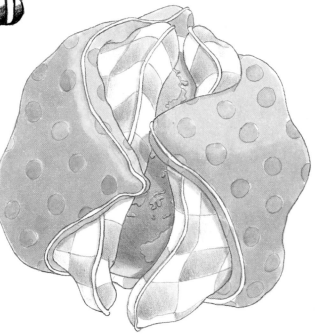

Global warming is like wrapping an extra blanket around Earth.

In the 1980s, there were all sorts of extreme weather conditions — heatwaves, droughts, floods, tornadoes, hurricanes, and typhoons — which some scientists have taken as a sign of global warming. Small changes in the average temperature or rainfall will make extreme events like these more frequent. This could be very dangerous. If, for example, an area has a drought for several years running, crops will fail and there will be famine. This is already happening in parts of Africa.

Global warming will be most noticeable in the polar regions. Ice caps will start to melt.

As ice caps melt, sea levels will rise. Places that are close to sea level, such as the Nile delta, will be underwater.

Scientists predict that the warming will not be spread evenly. The tropics will become only a little warmer, but the temperature at the North and South Poles may become up to 14°F (8°C) hotter. Any change in the way heat is spread around the world will upset where rain falls and how winds blow.

In a warmer world, more water will evaporate from the oceans, creating more rain and storms near the coasts. But farther inland, moisture evaporating from soils during hot summers will dry out fields and may cause crops to fail. Two of the major grain-growing areas — the midwestern United States and the Ukraine in the Soviet Union — are far inland and so are vulnerable. Warmer weather may, however, help farming in places now too cold to grow good crops, such as Siberia and northern Canada.

Places where much of the world's food is grown could become barren deserts if rains fail and soils dry out.

The oceans will absorb some of the extra heat from the air. But, since water expands as it warms, the sea level will rise. Ice caps and glaciers will melt, adding to the water in the oceans and making sea levels rise even farther. A rise of 3 feet (1 meter) in the next century would flood coastlines and low-lying land, where millions of people live. Salty water will make the surrounding land unsuitable for growing crops. Many of the world's great cities that are built by the sea, such as New York, London, Shanghai, and Sydney, could be flooded.

Spreading deserts and rising tides could leave millions of people hungry and homeless, especially in poor countries. Where will these environmental refugees go?

If the Antarctic ice caps totally melted, the sea level would rise as much as 195 feet. But this would take many hundreds of years.

25

TROUBLE IN THE AIR

The atmosphere is not only becoming warmer, it is also becoming dirtier. Car exhaust is mainly to blame, but so are power plants and factories. The fossil fuels they burn give off dangerous gases, which can cause diseases. The pollution is often worse in summer, when sunlight changes the gases into thin hazy clouds, called smog.

Polluting chemicals combine with water droplets in the air to form acid rain.

Some of the gases, nitrogen and sulphur dioxide in particular, float up into the clouds. There, the pure water droplets absorb the gases and turn into acid. These droplets eventually fall to Earth as acid rain. The acid rain can fall thousands of miles away from the source of the pollution.

Acid rain upsets the balance of minerals in the soil. It dissolves some — such as calcium and magnesium — which plants need, and releases other harmful ones, such as aluminum. Fir trees, in particular, are badly affected by acid rain. The needles develop yellow spots and drop off; the branches grow thin; the roots are damaged; and eventually the trees die.

Acid rain may wash into rivers and lakes, killing fish and other water creatures. Some lakes are so acidic that very little can survive in them.

Millions of conifers in Europe and North America have died as a result of acid rain.

The good news is that many countries now have laws to help clean up the air. Cleaner power plants mean less acidic rain. And all new cars are required to have special pollution-control devices on their exhaust pipes.

Snails and crayfish are the first to die as water becomes more acidic, followed by salmon and trout. Only eels can live in very acidic water.

Acid rain is as acidic as lemon juice and eats away at stone and metal. Millions of dollars are spent each year repairing damage to ornate cathedral stonework.

Air pollution is also damaging the ozone layer, which shields us from harmful ultraviolet radiation from the Sun. The damage is caused mainly by CFCs.

CFCs were thought to be very safe chemicals because they do not normally burn, decompose, or change in any way. Unfortunately, they *are* broken down by ultraviolet light. Sooner or later, the CFCs drift up through the atmosphere until they reach the ozone layer where the ultraviolet radiation is stronger. The radiation breaks up CFCs and chlorine is released. The chlorine reacts with the ozone and destroys it.

In the spring of 1984, scientists discovered a huge hole in the ozone layer over the frozen continent of Antarctica. In 1989, scientists also found a hole over the North Pole. The ozone layer is growing thinner in other places as well.

The hole in the ozone layer is like a crack in Earth's sunglasses, letting through harmful ultraviolet radiation.

The algae that live in the sea are sensitive to ultraviolet radiation and could be killed if the ozone layer gets too thin. This would be disastrous for other sea creatures, which eat algae. The entire food chain would be disrupted.

Now that people realize the damage done by CFCs, some countries have banned their use and asked factories to stop producing them. Most aerosol spray cans no longer contain CFCs, and scientists are looking for ways to replace them in other products too.

TIME FOR ACTION

Can you now see how all the pieces fit together? Earth is like a jigsaw puzzle. The land, sea, air and living things are all connected. By poisoning the water, destroying soils, killing off animals and plants, burning forests and polluting the air, it is as if we are throwing away some of the jigsaw pieces. That affects every inch of the planet.

But we need not despair. If we imagine the entire history of Earth so far lasting a single day, then humanlike creatures have been around for less than an hour, and Homo sapiens for less than a second. We are a very minor nuisance for a planet that has survived all kinds of major disasters.

Nature will survive. Even in the most polluted cities or rivers, some things can still live. What we have to worry about is whether we are making the world unfit for *us* to live on. Will the greenhouse effect turn our planet into an unbearably hot desert? Are we destroying the species of plants and animals that could feed and cure us in the future? Can we save the ozone layer which protects us?

Humans may be the most destructive species on the planet, but we do have one great advantage over other creatures: we can become aware of what we are doing to our environment and can work out ways to save it. Many countries are already cleaning up their rivers and stopping the pollution that causes acid rain. The world's governments joined together to act quickly once there was scientific proof that pollution was creating a hole in the ozone layer. There are plans for international action to halt the destruction of the rainforests and to find ways to slow down the greenhouse effect.

But we can't just leave things to governments. We must all help. You may think that you can't possibly make a difference to the crisis facing Earth. But you *can*. Remember, many of the problems we now face were caused by the individual actions of millions of people all over Earth. So each of us can help improve the environment. If each of us does what he or she can, Earth will be safe for future generations to enjoy. It's up to us.

Ways you can help

The first step is learning more about our planet's environmental problems and the possible solutions. Below are some books and magazines you may want to read and several organizations you can join. Pick a few of the organizations that interest you the most and write to them with your questions. Ask if they have any special programs or information for kids. You can help make Earth a safer, healthier and greener place to live!

Books and magazines

A Kid's Guide to
   How to Save the Planet
by Billy Goodman
Avon Books: 1990

50 Simple Things Kids Can Do
   to Save the Earth
by The Earth Works Group
Andrews and McMeel: 1990

Global Warming: Assessing
   the Greenhouse Threat
by Laurence Pringle
Arcade: 1990

Going Green: A Kid's
   Handbook to
   Saving the Planet
by John Elkington,
Julia Hailes, Douglas Hill
and Joel Makower
Puffin: 1990

P3 The Earth-Based Magazine for Kids
P. O. Box 52
Montgomery, VT 05470

Rainforest Secrets
by Arthur Dorros
Scholastic: 1990

Organizations

Greenpeace USA, Inc.
1436 U Street NW
Washington, DC 20009
(202) 462-1177

Center for Marine Conservation, Inc.
1725 DeSales St. NW, Suite 500
Washington, DC 20036
(202) 429-5609

Clean Water Action Project
1320 18th St. NW, 3rd floor
Washington, DC 20036
(202) 457-1286

Children of the Green Earth
Box 95219
Seattle, WA 98145
(no phone)

Hug the Earth
P. O. Box 621
Wayne, PA 19087
(215) 688-0566

The Acid Rain Foundation
1410 Varsity Drive
Raleigh, NC 27606
(919) 828-9443

Defenders of Wildlife
1244 19th St. NW
Washington, DC 20036
(202) 659-9510

Rainforest Alliance
270 Lafayette St., Suite 512
New York, NY 10012
(212) 941-1900

Kids Against Pollution
P. O. Box 775
Closter, NJ 07264
(201) 797-6800

Trees for Life
1103 Jefferson
Wichita, KS 67203
(316) 263-7294

Mothers and Others/NRDC
(National Resources Defense Council)
40 West 20th St.
New York, NY 10011
(212) 727-2700

National Wildlife Federation
1400 16th St. NW
Washington, DC 20036-266
(202) 797-6800

The Conservation Foundation
1250 24th St. NW
Washington, DC 20037
(202) 293-4800

Renew America
1001 Connecticut Ave. NW, Suite 1719
Washington, DC 20036
(202) 232-2252

First published in 1991 by
Kingfisher Books,
Grisewood & Dempsey Ltd.

Text copyright © 1991 by Fred Pearce
Illustrations copyright © 1991 by Ian Winton
Foreword copyright © 1991 by James Lovelock
All rights reserved.
First published in the United States by
Grosset & Dunlap, Inc., a member of
The Putnam & Grosset Book Group, New York.
Library of Congress Catalog Card Number: 90-84673
ISBN 0-448-40142-8
A B C D E F G H I J

Editor: Ruth Thomson
Assistant Editor: Karen Filsell
Art Director: Steve Avery
Designer: Roger Hands

Created and produced by
David Bennett Books Ltd.
94 Victoria Street, St Albans,
Herts, AL1 3TG

Typesetting by Type City
Production by Imago
Printed in Hong Kong